THE *Beauty* WITHIN

© 2009 Lake House Gifts
A Division of Ellie Claire Gift & Paper Corp.
www.ellieclaire.com

Compiled by Joanie Garborg
Designed by Lisa & Jeff Franke

All rights reserved. No part of this book may be reproduced in any form
without permission in writing from the publisher.

Scripture references are from the following sources: The Holy Bible, New International Version® NIV®. © 1973, 1978, 1984 by International Bible Society. Used by permission of Zondervan. The NEW AMERICAN STANDARD BIBLE® (NASB), © Copyright The Lockman Foundation 1960, 1962, 1963, 1968, 1971, 1972, 1973, 1975, 1977, 1995. Used by permission. (www.Lockman.org). The New King James Version® (NKJV). Copyright © 1982 by Thomas Nelson, Inc. Used by permission. The Holy Bible, New Living Translation® (NLT). Copyright © 1996, 2004. Used by permission of Tyndale House Publishers, Inc., Wheaton, Illinois. The Message © 1993, 1994, 1995, 1996, 2000, 2001, 2002 by Eugene Peterson. Used by permission of NavPress, Colorado Springs, CO. The Living Bible (TLB) © 1971 by permission of Tyndale House Publishers, Inc., Wheaton, Illinois. All rights reserved.

Excluding Scripture verses, references to men and masculine pronouns
have been replaced with gender-neutral references.

ISBN 978-1-935416-41-8
Printed in China

A WOMAN'S JOURNAL

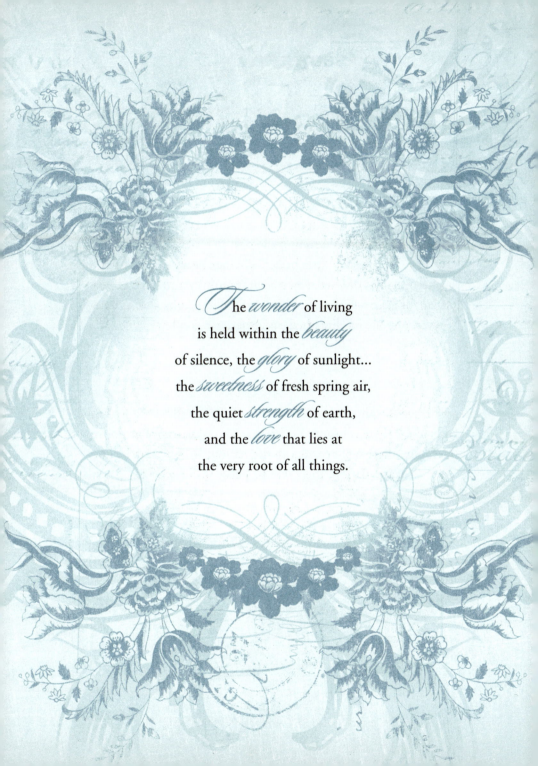

The *wonder* of living
is held within the *beauty*
of silence, the *glory* of sunlight...
the *sweetness* of fresh spring air,
the quiet *strength* of earth,
and the *love* that lies at
the very root of all things.

Beauty of Character

To appreciate beauty; to find the best in others; to give one's self; to leave the world a little better, whether by a healthy child, a garden patch, or a redeemed social condition; to have played and laughed with enthusiasm, and sung with exultation; to know even one life has breathed easier because you have lived... This is to have succeeded.

RALPH WALDO EMERSON

If there is righteousness in the heart, there will be beauty in the character. If there is beauty in the character, if there is harmony in the home, there will be order in the nation. When there is order in the nation, there will be peace in the world.

CHINESE PROVERB

Peace within makes beauty without.

ENGLISH PROVERB

Beauty of Character

Character strengthens our confident expectation of salvation. And this hope will not lead to disappointment. For we know how dearly God loves us.

ROMANS 5:4-5 NLT

A Place for Dreams

Hold fast your dreams!
Within your heart
Keep one still, secret spot
Where dreams may go
And, sheltered so,
May thrive and grow
Where doubt and fear are not.
O keep a place apart,
Within your heart,
For little dreams to go!

Louise Driscoll

God created us with an overwhelming desire to soar.
Our desire to develop and use every ounce of potential
He's placed in us is not egotistical. He designed us to be
tremendously productive and "to mount up with wings like eagles,"
realistically dreaming of what He can do with our potential.

Carol Kent

A Place for Dreams

When dreams come true at last, there is life and joy.

Proverbs 13:12 TLB

The Majesty of God

Honor and majesty surround Him;
strength and beauty fill His sanctuary.

PSALM 57:5 NLT

O Lord, our Lord, how majestic is Your name in all the earth!
You have set your glory above the heavens.... When I consider
Your heavens, the work of Your fingers, the moon and the stars,
which You have set in place, what is man that You are mindful of him,
the son of man that You care for him? You made him a little lower
than the heavenly beings and crowned him with glory and honor....
O Lord, our Lord, how majestic is Your name in all the earth!

PSALM 8:1, 3-5, 9 NIV

The Majesty of God

It was God who first set the stars in space; He is their Maker and Master—they are all in His hands and subject to His will. Such are His power and His majesty. Behold your God!

J. I. PACKER

Delight in the Lord

Take delight in the Lord, and He will give you your
heart's desires. Commit everything you do to the Lord.
Trust Him, and He will help you. He will make your
innocence radiate like the dawn, and the justice of
your cause will shine like the noonday sun.

PSALM 37:4-6 NLT

Send forth Your light and Your truth, let them guide me;
let them bring me to Your holy mountain,
to the place where You dwell. Then will I go to the
altar of God, to God, my joy and my delight.

PSALM 43:3-4 NIV

Delight in the Lord

Our fulfillment comes in knowing God's glory, loving Him for it, and delighting in it.

Special Plans

This is the real gift: you have been given the breath of life, designed with a unique, one-of-a-kind soul that exists forever—the way that you choose to live it doesn't change the fact that you've been given the gift of being now and forever. Priceless in value, you are handcrafted by God, who has a personal design and plan for each of us.

May God's love guide you through the special plans
He has for your life.

Allow your dreams a place in your prayers and plans. God-given dreams can help you move into the future He is preparing for you.

Special Plans

The Lord will work out His plans for my life—
for Your faithful love, O Lord, endures forever.

PSALM 138:8 NLT

Wonderful Love

Show the wonder of Your great love.... Keep me as the apple of Your eye; hide me in the shadow of Your wings.

PSALM 17:7-8 NIV

Give thanks to the Lord, for He is good! His faithful love endures forever.

PSALM 136:1 NLT

The Lord is merciful and compassionate, slow to get angry and filled with unfailing love. The Lord is good to everyone. He showers compassion on all His creation.... The Lord always keeps His promises; He is gracious in all He does.

PSALM 145:8-9, 13 NLT

Wonderful Love

> *Every one of us as human beings is known and loved by the Creator apart from every other human on earth.*
>
> — JAMES DOBSON

Windows of the Soul

Open wide the windows of our spirits and fill us full of light;
open wide the door of our hearts that we may receive and entertain
Thee with all the powers of our adoration.

CHRISTINA ROSSETTI

Faith goes up the stairs that love has made and looks out
the window which hope has opened.

CHARLES H. SPURGEON

Day-to-day living becomes a window through
which we get a glimpse of life eternal. The eternal
illuminates and gives focus to the daily.

JANICE RIGGLE HUIE

Windows of the Soul

All the earth shall be filled with the glory of the Lord.

NUMBERS 14:21 NKJV

Your thoughts—how rare, how beautiful!
God, I'll never comprehend them!
I couldn't even begin to count them—
any more than I could count the sand of the sea.
Oh, let me rise in the morning
and live always with You!

PSALM 139:17-18 THE MESSAGE

The Love of God

Can anything ever separate us from Christ's love? Does it mean He no longer loves us if we have trouble or calamity, or are persecuted, or hungry, or destitute, or in danger, or threatened with death?... No, despite all these things, overwhelming victory is ours through Christ, who loved us. And I am convinced that nothing can ever separate us from God's love. Neither death nor life, neither angels nor demons, neither our fears for today nor our worries about tomorrow—not even the powers of hell can separate us from God's love. No power in the sky above or in the earth below—indeed, nothing in all creation will ever be able to separate us from the love of God that is revealed in Christ Jesus our Lord.

ROMANS 8:35, 37-39 NLT

The Love of God

> The grace of God means:... Here is the world. Beautiful and terrible things will happen. Don't be afraid. I am with you. Nothing can ever separate us. It's for you I created the universe. I love you.
>
> FREDERICK BUECHNER

In His Image

God's designs regarding you, and His methods of bringing about these designs, are infinitely wise.

MADAME JEANNE GUYON

Stand outside this evening. Look at the stars. Know that you are special and loved by the One who created them.

All that we have and are is one of the unique and never-to-be repeated ways God has chosen to express Himself in space and time. Each of us, made in His image and likeness, is yet another promise He has made to the universe that He will continue to love it and care for it.

BRENNAN MANNING

In His Image

So God created human beings in His own image; In the image of God He created them; male and female He created them.

Genesis 1:27 NLT

Love One Another

Clothe yourselves with compassion, kindness, humility, gentleness and patience. Bear with each other and forgive whatever grievances you may have against one another. Forgive as the Lord forgave you. And over all these virtues put on love, which binds them all together in perfect unity.

COLOSSIANS 3:12-14 NIV

Don't just pretend to love others. Really love them. Hate what is wrong. Hold tightly to what is good. Love each other with genuine affection, and take delight in honoring each other.

ROMANS 12:9-10 NLT

May God who gives patience, steadfastness, and encouragement help you live in complete harmony with each other.

ROMANS 15:5 TLB

Love One Another

> *In God's wisdom, He frequently chooses to meet our needs by showing His love toward us through the hands and hearts of others.*
>
> — JACK HAYFORD

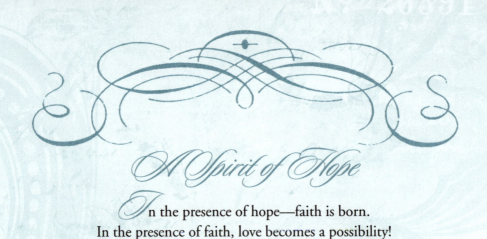

A Spirit of Hope

In the presence of hope—faith is born.
In the presence of faith, love becomes a possibility!
In the presence of love—miracles happen!

ROBERT SCHULLER

Hope floods my heart with delight!
Running on air, mad with life, dizzy, reeling,
Upward I mount—faith is sight, life is feeling,
Hope is the day-star of might!

MARGARET WITTER FULLER

Because You live, O Christ,
the spirit bird of hope is freed for flying,
our cages of despair no longer keep us
closed and life-denying.

SHIRLEY ERENA MURRAY

A Spirit of Hope

I pray that God, the source of hope, will fill you completely with joy and peace because you trust in Him. Then you will overflow with confident hope through the power of the Holy Spirit.

ROMANS 15:13 NLT

God-Provision

Has anyone by fussing before the mirror ever gotten taller by so much as an inch? If fussing can't even do that, why fuss at all? Walk into the fields and look at the wildflowers. They don't fuss with their appearance— but have you ever seen color and design quite like it? The ten best-dressed men and women in the country look shabby alongside them. If God gives such attention to the wildflowers, most of them never even seen, don't you think He'll attend to you, take pride in you, do His best for you?

LUKE 12:25-28 THE MESSAGE

Seek the Kingdom of God above all else, and He will give you everything you need. So don't be afraid, little flock. For it gives your Father great happiness to give you the Kingdom.

LUKE 12:31-32 NLT

God-Provision

At the very heart of the universe is God's desire to give.

Dreams Fulfilled

Lift up your eyes. Your heavenly Father waits to bless you—
in inconceivable ways to make your life what you
never dreamed it could be.

ANNE ORTLUND

The human heart, has hidden treasures,
In secret kept, in silence sealed;—
The thoughts, the hopes, the dreams, the pleasures,
Whose charms were broken if revealed.

CHARLOTTE BRONTË

Far away, there in the sunshine, are my highest aspirations.
I may not reach them but I can look up and see their beauty,
believe in them, and try to follow where they lead.

LOUISA MAY ALCOTT

Dreams Fulfilled

*I'll lead you to buried treasures, secret caches of valuables—
Confirmations that it is, in fact, I, God...who calls you by your name.*

ISAIAH 45:3 THE MESSAGE

Rest in Him

My soul finds rest in God alone; my salvation comes from Him.
He alone is my rock and my salvation; He is my fortress,
I will never be shaken.... My salvation and my honor depend on God;
He is my mighty rock, my refuge. Trust in Him at all times,
O people; pour out your hearts to Him, for God is our refuge....
One thing God has spoken, two things have I heard: that You,
O God, are strong, and that You, O Lord, are loving.

PSALM 62:1-2,7-8,11-12 NIV

Rest in the Lord, and wait patiently for Him.

PSALM 37:7 NKJV

Rest in Him

*When God finds a soul that rests in Him and is not easily moved...
to this same soul He gives the joy of His presence.*

CATHERINE OF GENOA

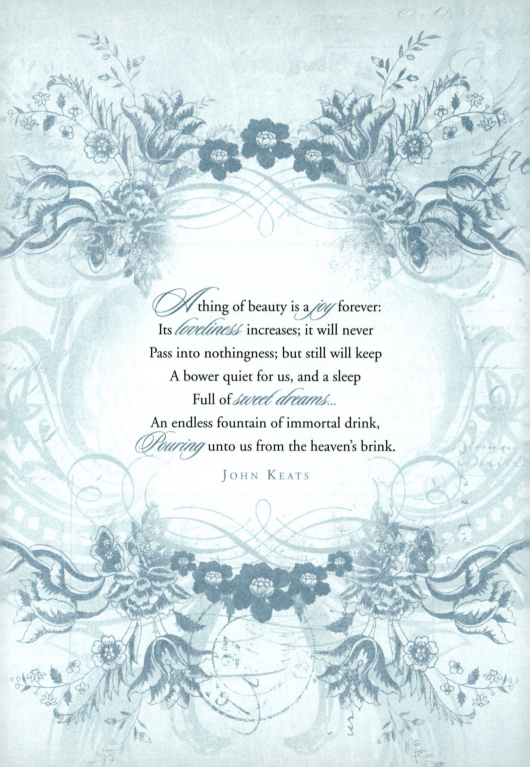

A thing of beauty is a *joy* forever:
Its *loveliness* increases; it will never
Pass into nothingness; but still will keep
A bower quiet for us, and a sleep
Full of *sweet dreams*...
An endless fountain of immortal drink,
Pouring unto us from the heaven's brink.

JOHN KEATS

Beauty Sought and Found

I have sought Thy nearness;
With all my heart have I called Thee,
And going out to meet Thee
I found Thee coming toward me.

Yehuda Halevi

If you are seeking after God, you may be sure of this: God is seeking you much more. He is the Lover, and you are His beloved. He has promised Himself to you.

John of the Cross

My Lord, You have heard the cry of my heart because it was You who cried out within my heart.

Thomas Merton

Beauty Sought and Found

Let us draw near to God with a sincere heart in full assurance of faith.... Let us hold unswervingly to the hope we profess, for He who promised is faithful.

HEBREWS 10:22-23 NIV

Love Like That

Watch what God does, and then you do it, like children who learn proper behavior from their parents. Mostly what God does is love you. Keep company with Him and learn a life of love. Observe how Christ loved us. His love was not cautious but extravagant. He didn't love in order to get something from us but to give everything of Himself to us. Love like that.

EPHESIANS 5:1-2 THE MESSAGE

I pray that your love will overflow more and more, and that you will keep on growing in your knowledge and understanding.

PHILIPPIANS 1:9 NLT

Love Like That

Open your hearts to the love God instills.... God loves you tenderly. What He gives you is not to be kept under lock and key, but to be shared.

MOTHER TERESA

God's Care

The Lord is my shepherd; I shall not want. He makes me to lie down in green pastures; He leads me beside the still waters. He restores my soul; He leads me in the paths of righteousness for His name's sake.

Yea, though I walk through the valley of the shadow of death, I will fear no evil; for You are with me; Your rod and Your staff, they comfort me. You prepare a table before me in the presence of my enemies; You anoint my head with oil; my cup runs over.

Surely goodness and mercy shall follow me all the days of my life; and I will dwell in the house of the Lord forever.

Psalm 23:1-6 NKJV

God's Care

God never abandons anyone on whom He has set His love; nor does Christ, the good shepherd, ever lose track of His sheep.

J. I. PACKER

The Little Things

It's the little things we do and say
That mean so much as we go our way.
A kindly deed can lift a load
From weary shoulders on the road.

A gentle word, like summer rain,
May soothe some heart and banish pain.
What joy or sadness often springs
From just the simple little things!

WILLA HOEY

Don't ever let yourself get so busy that you miss those little but important extras in life—the beauty of a day...the smile of a friend... the serenity of a quiet moment alone. For it is often life's smallest pleasures and gentlest joys that make the biggest and most lasting difference.

It's the little things that make up the richest part
of the tapestry of our lives.

The Little Things

> He won't brush aside the bruised and the hurt and He won't disregard the small and insignificant, but He'll steadily and firmly set things right.
>
> ISAIAH 42:3 THE MESSAGE

Of Great Value

Are not five sparrows sold for two cents? Yet not one of them is forgotten before God. Indeed, the very hairs of your head are all numbered. Do not fear; you are more valuable than many sparrows.

LUKE 12:6-7 NASB

For God bought you with a high price. So you must honor God with your body.

1 CORINTHIANS 6:20 NLT

For you know that it was not with perishable things such as silver or gold that you were redeemed...but with the precious blood of Christ, a lamb without blemish or defect.

1 PETER 1:18-19 NIV

Of Great Value

You are in the Beloved...therefore infinitely dear to the Father, unspeakably precious to Him.

NORMAN F. DOWTY

The Goodness of God

The goodness of God is infinitely more wonderful than we will ever be able to comprehend.

A. W. TOZER

All that is good, all that is true, all that is beautiful, all that is beneficent, be it great or small, be it perfect or fragmentary, natural as well as supernatural, moral as well as material, comes from God.

JOHN HENRY NEWMAN

We walk without fear, full of hope and courage and strength to do His will, waiting for the endless good which He is always giving as fast as He can get us able to take it in.

GEORGE MACDONALD

The Goodness of God

Open your mouth and taste, open your eyes and see—how good God is. Blessed are you who run to Him. Worship God if you want the best; worship opens doors to all His goodness.

PSALM 34:8-9 THE MESSAGE

Messages of Beauty

In the central place of every heart, there is a recording chamber; so long as it receives messages of beauty, hope, cheer, and courage, so long you are young.

DOUGLAS MACARTHUR

Cheerfulness keeps up a kind of daylight in the mind, and fills it with a steady and perpetual serenity.

JOSEPH ADDISON

Some days, it is enough encouragement just to watch the clouds break up and disappear, leaving behind a blue patch of sky and bright sunshine that is so warm upon my face. It's a glimpse of divinity; a kiss from heaven.

Women are beautiful, every single one of us. It is one of the glorious ways that we bear the image of God.

STASI ELDREDGE

May gentle and beautiful moments be yours today.

Messages of Beauty

He has made everything beautiful in its time.

ECCLESIASTES 3:11 NIV

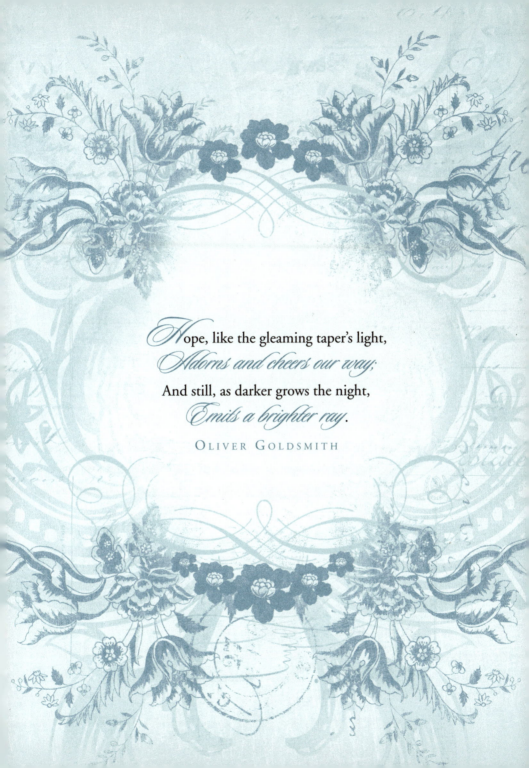

Hope, like the gleaming taper's light,
Adorns and cheers our way;
And still, as darker grows the night,
Emits a brighter ray.

OLIVER GOLDSMITH

God Is Our Refuge

Hear my cry, O God; Give heed to my prayer. From the end of the earth I call to You when my heart is faint; lead me to the rock that is higher than I. For You have been a refuge for me, a tower of strength against the enemy. Let me dwell in Your tent forever; let me take refuge in the shelter of Your wings.

PSALM 61:1-4 NASB

Whom have I in heaven but You? And besides You, I desire nothing on earth. My flesh and my heart may fail, but God is the strength of my heart and my portion forever.... As for me, the nearness of God is my good; I have made the Lord God my refuge.

PSALM 73:25-26, 28 NASB

God Is Our Refuge

When God has become...our refuge and our fortress, then we can reach out to Him in the midst of a broken world and feel at home while still on the way.

HENRI J. M. NOUWEN

Enfolded in Peace

I will let God's peace infuse every part of today. As the chaos swirls and life's demands pull at me on all sides, I will breathe in God's peace that surpasses all understanding. He has promised that He would set within me a peace too deeply planted to be affected by unexpected or exhausting demands.

Calm me, O Lord, as you stilled the storm,
Still me, O Lord, keep me from harm.
Let all the tumult within me cease,
Enfold me, Lord, in your peace.

CELTIC TRADITIONAL

God cannot give us a happiness and peace apart from Himself, because it is not there. There is no such thing.

C. S. LEWIS

Enfolded in Peace

Because of the tender mercy of our God, with which the Sunrise from on high will visit us, to shine upon those who sit in darkness… to guide our feet into the way of peace.

LUKE 1:78-79 NASB

Protection

The Lord is my light and my salvation—whom shall I fear? The Lord is the stronghold of my life—of whom shall I be afraid?... One thing I ask of the Lord, this is what I seek: that I may dwell in the house of the Lord all the days of my life, to gaze upon the beauty of the Lord and to seek Him in His temple. For in the day of trouble He will keep me safe in His dwelling; He will hide me in the shelter of His tabernacle and set me high upon a rock.... Hear my voice when I call, O Lord; be merciful to me and answer me. My heart says of you, "Seek His face!" Your face, Lord, I will seek.

Psalm 27:1, 4-5, 7-8 NIV

Protection

Leave behind your fear and dwell on the lovingkindness of God, that you may recover by gazing on Him.

The Beauty of Dreams

We grow great by dreams.... [We] see things in the soft haze of a spring day or in the red fire of a long winter's evening. Some of us let these great dreams die, but others nourish and protect them; nurse them through bad days till they bring them to the sunshine and light, which comes always to those who sincerely hope that their dreams will come true.

WOODROW WILSON

The future belongs to those who believe
in the beauty of their dreams.

ELEANOR ROOSEVELT

God gives us dreams so we'll long for His reality.

BETH MOORE

The Beauty of Dreams

Trust steadily in God, hope unswervingly, love extravagantly.

1 CORINTHIANS 13:13 THE MESSAGE

God's Thoughts

How great are Your works, O Lord,
how profound Your thoughts!

PSALM 92:5 NIV

The Lord is the everlasting God, the Creator of all the earth. He never grows weak or weary. No one can measure the depths of His understanding.... Even youths will become weak and tired, and young men will fall in exhaustion. But those who trust in the Lord will find new strength. They will soar high on wings like eagles. They will run and not grow weary. They will walk and not faint.

ISAIAH 40:28, 30-31 NLT

God's Thoughts

Just when we least expect it, [God] intrudes into our neat and tidy notions about who He is and how He works.

JONI EARECKSON TADA

Child of God

When we call on God, He bends down His ear to listen,
as a father bends down to listen to his little child.

ELIZABETH CHARLES

He only is the Maker
of all things near and far;
He paints the wayside flower,
He lights the evening star;
the wind and waves obey Him,
by Him the birds are fed;
much more to us, His children,
He gives our daily bread.

MATTHIAS CLAUDIUS

Remember you are very special to God as His precious child.
He has promised to complete the good work He has
begun in you. As you continue to grow in Him,
He will make you a blessing to others.

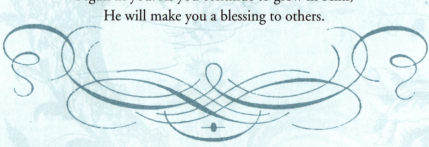

Child of God

> *How great is the love the Father has lavished on us, that we should be called children of God! And that is what we are!*
>
> 1 JOHN 3:1 NIV

In the Sunshine

See each morning a world made anew, as if it were the
morning of the very first day;...treasure and use it,
as if it were the final hour of the very last day.

FAY HARTZELL ARNOLD

Go outside, to the fields, enjoy nature and the sunshine, go out
and try to recapture happiness in yourself and in God. Think of
all the beauty that's still left in and around you and be happy!

ANNE FRANK

The beauty of the earth, the beauty of the sky, the order of
the stars, the sun, the moon...their very loveliness is their
confession of God: for who made these lovely mutable things,
but He who is Himself unchangeable beauty?

AUGUSTINE

In the Sunshine

May they who love you be like the sun when it rises in its strength.

JUDGES 5:31 NIV

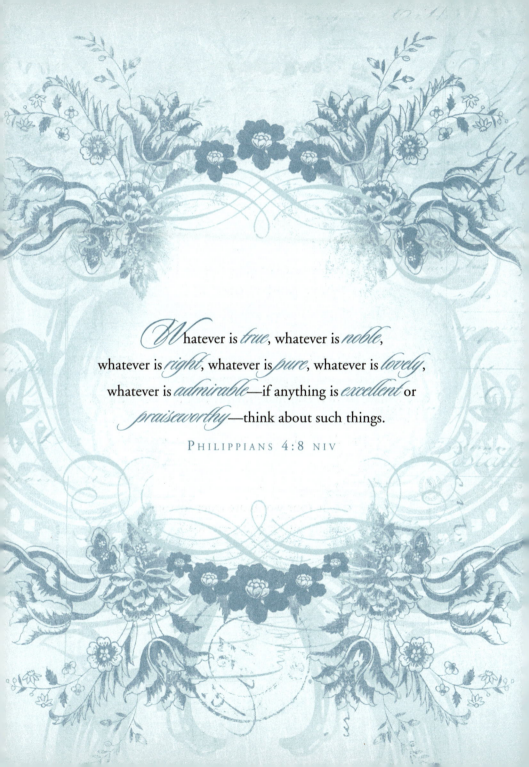

Whatever is true, whatever is noble, whatever is right, whatever is pure, whatever is lovely, whatever is admirable—if anything is excellent or praiseworthy—think about such things.

PHILIPPIANS 4:8 NIV

Renewing Word

You're my place of quiet retreat; I wait for
Your Word to renew me.

PSALM 119:114 THE MESSAGE

You have dealt well with Your servant, O Lord, according to
Your word. Teach me good judgment and knowledge,
for I believe in Your commandments. Before I was afflicted
I went astray, but now I keep Your word. You are good,
and do good; teach me Your statutes.

PSALM 119:65-68 NKJV

All Your words are true; all Your
righteous laws are eternal.

PSALM 119:160 NIV

Renewing Word

Be still, and in the quiet moments, listen to the voice of your heavenly Father. His words can renew your spirit... no one knows you and your needs like He does.

JANET L. WEAVER SMITH

Special Gifts

Every person ever created is so special that their presence in the world makes it richer and fuller and more wonderful than it could ever have been without them.

We were not sent into this world to do anything into which we cannot put our hearts.

JOHN RUSKIN

Use what talents you possess: the woods would be very silent if no birds sang there except those that sang best.

HENRY VAN DYKE

All the beautiful sentiments in the world weigh less than a simple lovely action.

JAMES RUSSELL LOWELL

God gives everyone a special gift and a special place to use it.

Special Gifts

*Where you are right now is God's place for you.
Live and obey and love and believe right there.*

1 CORINTHIANS 7:17 THE MESSAGE

Perfect Peace

Don't worry about anything; instead, pray about everything. Tell God what you need, and thank Him for all He has done. Then you will experience God's peace, which exceeds anything we can understand. His peace will guard your hearts and minds as you live in Christ Jesus.

PHILIPPIANS 4:6-7 NLT

You will keep in perfect peace him whose mind is steadfast, because he trusts in You. Trust in the Lord forever, for the Lord, the Lord, is the Rock eternal.

ISAIAH 26:3-4 NIV

Therefore, having been justified by faith, we have peace with God through our Lord Jesus Christ.

ROMANS 5:1 NKJV

Perfect Peace

> The God of peace gives perfect peace to those
> whose hearts are stayed upon Him.
>
> CHARLES H. SPURGEON

Full of Laughter

Teach me, Father, to value each day, to live, to love, to laugh, to play.

KATHI MILLS

Wholehearted, ready laughter heals, encourages, relaxes anyone within hearing distance. The laughter that springs from love makes wide the space around it—gives room for the loved one to enter in. Real laughter welcomes, and never shuts out.

EUGENIA PRICE

Sense of humor; God's great gift
causes spirits to uplift,
Helps to make our bodies mend;
lightens burdens; cheers a friend;
Tickles children; elders grin
at this warmth that glows within;
Surely in the great hereafter
heaven must be full of laughter!

It is often just as sacred to laugh as it is to pray.

CHARLES R. SWINDOLL

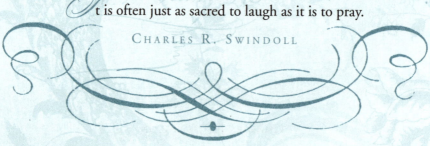

Full of Laughter

*He will yet fill your mouth with laughter
and your lips with shouts of joy.*

JOB 8:21 NIV

Powerful and Faithful

Search high and low, scan skies and land, you'll find nothing and no one quite like God. The holy angels are in awe before Him; He looms immense and august over everyone around Him. God-of-the-Angel-Armies, who is like You, powerful and faithful from every angle?

PSALM 89:6-8 THE MESSAGE

Yours, O Lord, is the greatness, the power, the glory, the victory, and the majesty. Everything in the heavens and on earth is Yours, O Lord, and this is Your kingdom. We adore You as the one who is over all things.

1 CHRONICLES 29:11 NLT

Ah Lord God! Behold, You have made the heavens and the earth by Your great power and Your outstretched arm! Nothing is too difficult for You.

JEREMIAH 32:17 NASB

Powerful and Faithful

*Whatever the circumstances, whatever the call...
His strength will be your strength in your hour of need.*

BILLY GRAHAM

Made for Joy

Our hearts were made for joy. Our hearts were made to enjoy the One who created them. Too deeply planted to be much affected by the ups and downs of life, this joy is a knowing and a being known by our Creator. He sets our hearts alight with radiant joy.

If one is joyful, it means that one is faithfully living for God, and that nothing else counts; and if one gives joy to others one is doing God's work. With joy without and joy within, all is well.

JANET ERSKINE STUART

Live for today but hold your hands open to tomorrow. Anticipate the future and its changes with joy. There is a seed of God's love in every event, every circumstance, every unpleasant situation in which you may find yourself.

BARBARA JOHNSON

The joy of the Lord is your strength.

NEHEMIAH 8:10 NKJV

Designed on Purpose

All the days ordained for me were written in
Your book before one of them came to be.

PSALM 139:16 NIV

It's in Christ that we find out who we are and what we are living for.
Long before we first heard of Christ and got our hopes up, He had
His eye on us, had designs on us for glorious living, part of the
overall purpose He is working out in everything and everyone.

EPHESIANS 1:11-12 THE MESSAGE

To everything there is a season, a time for
every purpose under heaven.

ECCLESIASTES 3:1 NKJV

The plans of the Lord stand firm forever, the purposes
of His heart through all generations.

PSALM 33:11 NIV

Designed on Purpose

The patterns of our days are always rearranging...and each design for living is unique, graced with its own special beauty.

There's not a tint that *paints the rose*
Or decks the lily fair,
Or marks the humblest flower that grows,
But *God has placed it there*....
There's not a place on earth's vast round,
In ocean's deep or air,
Where love and beauty are not found,
For God is *everywhere*.

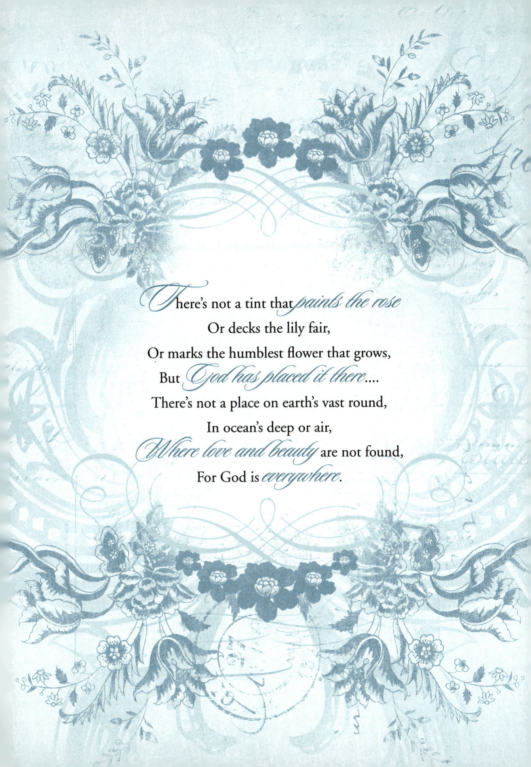

Faith Adventure

There will always be the unknown. There will always be the unprovable. But faith confronts those frontiers with a thrilling leap. Then life becomes vibrant with adventure!

ROBERT SCHULLER

Faith means you want God and want to want nothing else.... In faith there is movement and development. Each day something is new.

BRENNAN MANNING

A little faith will bring your soul to heaven, but a lot of faith will bring heaven to your soul.

DWIGHT L. MOODY

Faith is not a sense, not sight, not reason, but a taking God at His Word.

EVANS

For with God all things are possible.

MARK 10:27 NKJV

The Garden of My Life

At that same time, a fine vineyard will appear. There's something to sing about! I, God, tend it. I keep it well-watered. I keep careful watch over it so that no one can damage it.... Even if it gives me thistles and thornbushes, I'll just pull them out and burn them up. Let that vine cling to me for safety, let it find a good and whole life with me, let it hold on for a good and whole life.

ISAIAH 27:2-5 THE MESSAGE

The Lord will guide you always; He will satisfy your needs in a sun-scorched land and will strengthen your frame. You will be like a well-watered garden, like a spring whose waters never fail.

ISAIAH 58:11 NIV

The Garden of My Life

It is God's knowledge of me, His careful husbanding of the ground of my being, His constant presence in the garden of my little life that guarantees my joy.

W. PHILLIP KELLER

New Every Morning

Morning has broken like the first morning,
Blackbird has spoken like the first bird....
Praise with elation, praise every morning,
God's re-creation of the new day!

ELEANOR FARJEON

Today is a new day. You will get out of it just what you put into it. If you have made mistakes, even serious mistakes, there is always another chance for you.... You may have a fresh start any moment you choose, for this thing we call "failure" is not the falling down, but the staying down.

MARY PICKFORD

That is God's call to us—simply to be people who are content to live close to Him and to renew the kind of life in which the closeness is felt and experienced.

THOMAS MERTON

New Every Morning

It is good to give thanks to the Lord and to sing praises to Your name, O Most High; to declare Your lovingkindness in the morning and Your faithfulness by night.

Psalm 92:1-2 NASB

The Right Word

Let everything you say be good and helpful, so that your words will be an encouragement to those who hear them.

EPHESIANS 4:29 NLT

Like apples of gold in settings of silver is a word spoken in right circumstances. Like an earring of gold and an ornament of fine gold is a wise reprover to a listening ear. Like the cold of snow in the time of harvest is a faithful messenger to those who send him.

PROVERBS 25:11-13 NASB

Whatever you do in word or deed, do all in the name of the Lord Jesus, giving thanks to God the Father through Him.

COLOSSIANS 3:17 NKJV

The Right Word

Walk softly. Speak tenderly. Love fervently.

God Draws Near

When you are lonely I wish you love;
When you are down I wish you joy;
When you are troubled I wish you peace;
When things are complicated I wish you simple beauty;
When things are chaotic I wish you inner silence;
When things seem empty I wish you hope,
And the sweet sense of God's presence every passing day.

God still draws near to us in the ordinary,
commonplace, everyday experiences and places....
He comes in surprising ways.

Henry Gariepy

In both simple and eloquent ways, our infinite God
personally reveals glimpses of Himself in the finite.

God Draws Near

I have set the Lord always before me; because He is at my right hand I shall not be moved.

PSALM 16:8 NKJV

Fear Not

Don't be afraid, I've redeemed you. I've called your name. You're mine. When you're in over your head, I'll be there with you. When you're in rough waters, you will not go down. When you're between a rock and a hard place, it won't be a dead end—Because I am God, your personal God, The Holy of Israel, your Savior. I paid a huge price for you...! *That's* how much you mean to me! *That's* how much I love you!

ISAIAH 43:1-4 THE MESSAGE

If God is for us, who can be against us?

ROMANS 8:31 NKJV

Fear Not

Nothing we can do will make the Father love us less; nothing we do can make Him love us more. He loves us unconditionally with an everlasting love.

NANCIE CARMICHAEL

I Found Loveliness

I found loveliness today
Down along life's broad highway—
Saw its beauty in the trees,
Heard it whisper in the breeze,
Listed it in songbird's trill,
Felt its warmth in glad sunshine,
Rhythm caught in swaying pine—
All along life's broad highway
I found loveliness today.

I found loveliness today
Down along life's broad highway—
Beauty within pastures green,
Next in clouds of silvery sheen,
Golden glow at break of day,
Joy in children at their play,
Scented odor of wild rose;
Peace I found where violet grows—
All along life's broad highway
I found loveliness today.

CARLTON EVERETT KNOX

I Found Loveliness

*How lovely are Your dwelling places, O Lord of hosts!
My soul longed and even yearned for the courts of the Lord.*

PSALM 84:1-2 NASB

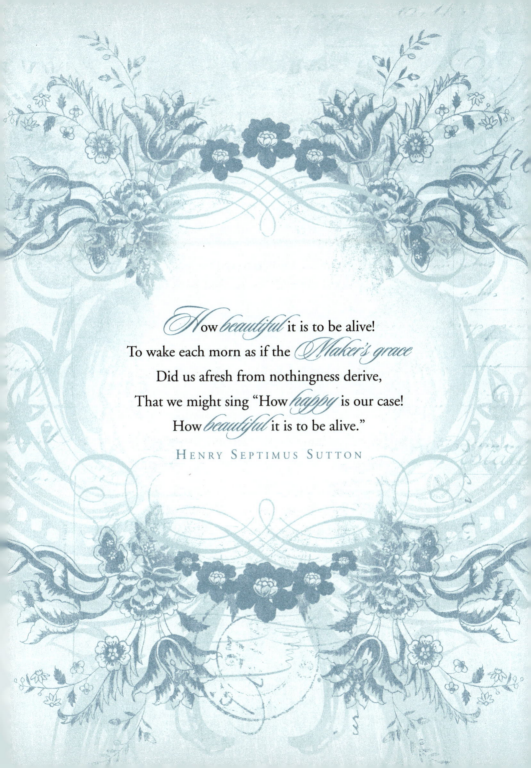

How beautiful it is to be alive!
To wake each morn as if the *Maker's grace*
Did us afresh from nothingness derive,
That we might sing "How *happy* is our case!
How *beautiful* it is to be alive."

HENRY SEPTIMUS SUTTON

Paths of Life

You have made known to me the paths of life;
You will fill me with joy in Your presence.

ACTS 2:28 NIV

But the path of the just is like the shining sun,
that shines ever brighter unto the perfect day.

PROVERBS 4:18 NKJV

Your word is a lamp to my feet and a light to my path.

PSALM 119:105 NASB

Come, and let us go up to the mountain of the Lord....
He will teach us of His ways, and we shall walk in His paths.

MICAH 4:2 NKJV

Paths of Life

....
....
....
....
....
....
....
....
....
....
....
....
....
....
....
....
....

The best things are nearest…light in your eyes, flowers at your feet, duties at your hand, the path of God just before you.

ROBERT LOUIS STEVENSON

Faith Is the Centerpiece

Faith does more than give reality to that which we do not see;
it makes us look differently at visible things.... Faith, as the Bible
defines it, is present-tense action. Faith means being sure of
what we hope for...now. It means knowing something is real,
this moment, all around you, even when you don't see it.
Great faith isn't the ability to believe long and far into the misty future.
It's simply taking God at His word and taking the next step.

JONI EARECKSON TADA

Faith is the centerpiece of a connected life.
It allows us to live by the grace of invisible strands.
It is a belief in a wisdom superior to our own.

TERRY TEMPEST WILLIAMS

Faith Is the Centerpiece

Because of Christ and our faith in Him, we can now come boldly and confidently into God's presence.

Ephesians 3:12 NLT

The Miracle of Friendship

There's a miracle called friendship
That dwells within the heart,
And you don't know how it happens
Or where it gets its start.
But the happiness it brings you
Always gives a special lift,
And you realize that friendship
Is life's most precious gift.

The first blush of friendship is a grace to behold: a moment of shyness, a tentative hello. Every other gift in life takes wing from here—affection, generosity, sharing—until soon your life is rich.

The impulse of love that leads us to the doorway of a friend is the voice of God within.

AGNES SANFORD

The Miracle of Friendship

A friend loves at all times.

PROVERBS 17:17 NKJV

Watchful Care

God takes care of His own. He knows our needs. He anticipates our crises. He is moved by our weaknesses. He stands ready to come to our rescue. And at just the right moment He steps in and proves Himself as our faithful heavenly Father.

Charles R. Swindoll

He paints the lily of the field,
Perfumes each lily bell;
If He so loves the little flowers,
I know He loves me well.

Maria Straus

God cares for the world He created, from the rising of a nation to the falling of the sparrow. Everything in the world lies under the watchful gaze of His providential eyes, from the numbering of the days of our life to the numbering of the hairs on our head.

Ken Gire

Watchful Care

> For He will give His angels charge concerning you,
> to guard you in all your ways.
>
> PSALM 91:11 NASB

God's Compassion

Through the Lord's mercies we are not consumed, because His compassions fail not. They are new every morning; great is Your faithfulness. "The Lord is my portion," says my soul, "Therefore I hope in Him." The Lord is good to them that wait for Him, to the soul that seeks Him.

Lamentations 3:22-25 nkjv

Lord, don't hold back Your tender mercies from me. Let Your unfailing love and faithfulness always protect me.

Psalm 40:11 nlt

You, O Lord, are a compassionate and gracious God, slow to anger, abounding in love and faithfulness.

Psalm 86:14-16 niv

God's Compassion

The loving God we serve has immeasurable compassion and tenderness toward each of us throughout our lives.

JAMES DOBSON

Happiness and Gratitude

It is not how much we have, but how much we enjoy, that makes happiness.

CHARLES H. SPURGEON

Life itself, every bit of health that we enjoy, every hour of liberty and free enjoyment, the ability to see, to hear, to speak, to think, and to imagine—all this comes from the hand of God. We show our gratitude by giving back to Him a part of that which He has given to us.

BILLY GRAHAM

Our inner happiness depends not on what we experience but on the degree of our gratitude to God, whatever the experience.

ALBERT SCHWEITZER

Happiness and Gratitude

*I will bless the Lord at all times;
His praise shall continually be in my mouth.*

PSALM 34:1 NKJV

An Undivided Heart

Above all else, guard your heart,
for it is the wellspring of life.

PROVERBS 4:23 NIV

I will give them an undivided heart and put a new spirit in them;
I will remove from them their heart of stone and give them a heart
of flesh. Then...they will be my people, and I will be their God.

EZEKIEL 11:19-20 NIV

"Love the Lord your God with all your heart, all your soul,
and all your mind." This is the first and greatest commandment.

MATTHEW 22:37-38 NLT

An Undivided Heart

In the deepest heart of everyone, God planted a longing for Himself as He is: a God of love.

EUGENIA PRICE

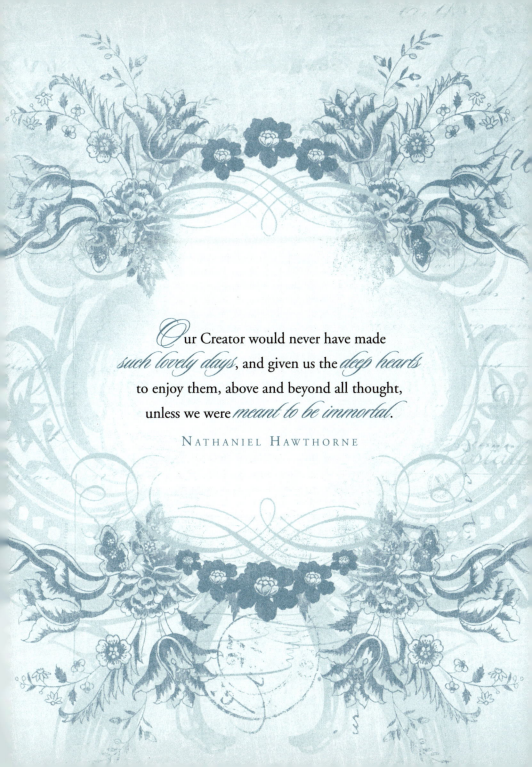

*O*ur Creator would never have made *such lovely days*, and given us the *deep hearts* to enjoy them, above and beyond all thought, unless we were *meant to be immortal*.

NATHANIEL HAWTHORNE

Glorious Handiwork

He made you so you could share in His creation,
could love and laugh and know Him.

TED GRIFFEN

You are a creation of God unequaled anywhere
in the universe.... Thank Him for yourself and then
for all the rest of His glorious handiwork.

NORMAN VINCENT PEALE

The huge dome of the sky is of all things sensuously
perceived the most like infinity. When God made space
and worlds that move in space, and clothed our world
with air, and gave us such eyes and such imaginations as
those we have, He knew what the sky would mean to us....
We cannot be certain that this was not indeed one
of the chief purposes for which Nature was created.

C. S. LEWIS

Glorious Handiwork

> The heavens declare His righteousness,
> and all the peoples see His glory.
>
> Psalm 97:6 NKJV

Daily Graces

Thank you, God, for little things
That often come our way,
The things we take for granted
But don't mention when we pray.

The unexpected courtesy,
The thoughtful kindly deed,
A hand reached out to help us
In the time of sudden need.

Oh, make us more aware, dear God,
Of little daily graces
That come to us with sweet surprise
From never-dreamed-of places.

To be grateful is to recognize the Love of God in everything
He has given us—and He has given us everything.
Every breath we draw is a gift of His love, every moment of existence
is a gift of grace, for it brings with it immense graces from Him.

—Thomas Merton

Daily Graces

Give us day by day our daily bread.

LUKE 11:3 NKJV

Abundant Life

I came so they can have real and eternal life,
more and better life than they ever dreamed of.

JOHN 10:10 THE MESSAGE

*I*n the beginning was the Word, and the Word was with God,
and the Word was God. He was in the beginning with God.
All things came into being through Him, and apart from
Him nothing came into being that has come into being.
In Him was life, and the life was the Light of men....
For of His fullness we have all received, and grace upon grace.

JOHN 1:1-4, 16 NASB

Abundant Life

> *He is looking for people who will come in simple dependence upon His grace.... At this very moment, He's looking at you.*
>
> — JACK HAYFORD

Unique Gifts

God has a wonderful plan for each person He has chosen. He knew even before He created this world what beauty He would bring forth from our lives.

LOUIS B. WYLY

Everyone has a unique role to fill in the world and is important in some respect. Everyone, including and perhaps especially you, is indispensable.

NATHANIEL HAWTHORNE

God gives us all gifts, special abilities that we are entrusted with developing to help serve Him and serve others.

Unique Gifts

God has given each of you some special abilities; be sure to use them to help each other, passing on to others God's many kinds of blessings.

1 Peter 4:10 TLB

Seek First

"ook at the birds of the air, that they do not sow, nor reap nor gather into barns, and yet your heavenly Father feeds them. Are you not worth much more than they? And who of you by being worried can add a single hour to his life?

And why are you worried about clothing? Observe how the lilies of the field grow; they do not toil nor do they spin, yet I say to you that not even Solomon in all his glory clothed himself like one of these. But if God so clothes the grass of the field, which is alive today and tomorrow is thrown into the furnace, will He not much more clothe you? You of little faith!

Do not worry then, saying, "What will we eat?" or "What will we drink?" or "What will we wear for clothing?" For...your heavenly Father knows that you need all these things. But seek first His kingdom and His righteousness, and all these things will be added to you.

MATTHEW 6:26-33 NASB

Seek First

> Trust the past to the mercy of God, the present to His love, and the future to His Providence.
>
> **Augustine**

The Warmth of Love

Though I have seen the oceans and mountains, though I have read great books and seen great works of art, though I have heard symphonies and tasted the best wines and foods, there is nothing greater or more beautiful than those people I love.

CHRISTOPHER DE VINCK

Not every day of our lives is overflowing with joy and celebration. But there are moments when our hearts nearly burst within us for the sheer joy of being alive. The first sight of our newborn babies, the warmth of love in another's eyes, the fresh scent of rain on a hot summer's eve—moments like these renew in us a heartfelt appreciation for life.

GWEN ELLIS

When one has once fully entered the realm of love, the world—no matter how imperfect—becomes rich and beautiful, for it consists solely of opportunities for love.

SØREN KIERKEGAARD

The Warmth of Love

All of you should be of one mind. Sympathize with each other. Love each other as brothers and sisters. Be tenderhearted, and keep a humble attitude.

1 Peter 3:8 NLT

Good Gifts

Every good gift and every perfect gift is from above,
and comes down from the Father of lights,
with whom is no variation or shadow of turning.

JAMES 1:17 NKJV

Rejoice in the Lord your God! For the rain He sends
demonstrates His faithfulness. Once more the
autumn rains will come, as well as the rains of spring.

JOEL 2:23 NLT

He has not left Himself without testimony: He has shown kindness
by giving you rain from heaven and crops in their seasons;
He provides you with plenty of food and fills your hearts with joy.

ACTS 14:17 NIV

Good Gifts

*All perfect gifts are from above and all our blessings show
The amplitude of God's dear love which any heart may know.*

LAURA LEE RANDALL

Late have I *loved* You,
O beauty so ancient and so new.
Late have *I loved You!*
You were within me
while I have gone outside *to seek You*.
Unlovely myself, I rushed
towards all those lovely things You had made.
And *always You were with me*.

AUGUSTINE

Indescribable Love

Could we with ink the ocean fill,
And were the skies of parchment made,
Were every stalk on earth a quill,
And every man a scribe by trade
To write the love of God above
Would drain the ocean dry,
Nor could the scroll contain the whole
Though stretched from sky to sky.

MEIR BEN ISAAC NEHORAI

Love is the response of the heart to the overwhelming goodness of God.... You may be so awestruck and full of love at His presence that words do not come.

RICHARD J. FOSTER

Indescribable Love

Thanks be to God for His indescribable gift!

2 Corinthians 9:15 NASB

A Personal Guide

I'll take the hand of those who don't know the way, who can't see where they're going. I'll be a personal guide to them, directing them through unknown country. I'll be right there to show them what roads to take, make sure they don't fall into the ditch. These are the things I'll be doing for them—sticking with them, not leaving them for a minute.

ISAIAH 42:16 THE MESSAGE

Whether you turn to the right or to the left, your ears will hear a voice behind you, saying, "This is the way; walk in it."

ISAIAH 30:21 NIV

We can make our plans, but the Lord determines our steps.

PROVERBS 16:9 NLT

A Personal Guide

Heaven often seems distant and unknown, but if He who made the road…is our guide, we need not fear to lose the way.

HENRY VAN DYKE

To Be Alive

It seems to me we can never give up longing and wishing while we are alive. There are certain things we feel to be beautiful and good, and we must hunger for them.

GEORGE ELIOT

It is the simple things of life that make living worthwhile, the sweet fundamental things such as love and duty, work and rest, and living close to nature.

LAURA INGALLS WILDER

Life is what we are alive to. It is not length but breadth.... Be alive to...goodness, kindness, purity, love, history, poetry, music, flowers, stars, God, and eternal hope.

MALTBIE D. BABCOCK

To Be Alive

The Lord will command His lovingkindness in the daytime; and His song will be with me in the night, a prayer to the God of my life.

PSALM 42:8 NASB

Wide Open Spaces

By entering through faith into what God has always wanted to do for us—set us right with Him, make us fit for Him—we have it all together with God because of our Master Jesus. And that's not all: We throw open our doors to God and discover at the same moment that He has already thrown open His door to us. We find ourselves standing where we always hoped we might stand—out in the wide open spaces of God's grace and glory, standing tall and shouting our praise.

ROMANS 5:1-2 THE MESSAGE

Wide Open Spaces

*Whoever walks toward God one step,
God runs toward him two.*

Go Out in Joy

You'll go out in joy, you'll be led into a whole and complete life. The mountains and hills will lead the parade, bursting with song. All the trees of the forest will join the procession, exuberant with applause.

ISAIAH 55:12 THE MESSAGE

You will make known to me the path of life; in Your presence is fullness of joy; in Your right hand there are pleasures forever.

PSALM 16:11 NASB

But let all who take refuge in You rejoice; let them sing joyful praises forever. Spread Your protection over them, that all who love Your name may be filled with joy. For You bless the godly, O Lord; You surround them with Your shield of love.

PSALM 5:11-12 NLT

Go Out in Joy

*Those who run in the path of God's commands
have their hearts set free.*

The Rhythms of Life

In waiting we begin to get in touch with the rhythms of life—stillness and action, listening and decision. They are the rhythms of God. It is in the everyday and the commonplace that we learn patience, acceptance, and contentment.

RICHARD J. FOSTER

Love comes while we rest against our Father's chest.
Joy comes when we catch the rhythms of His heart.
Peace comes when we live in harmony with those rhythms.

KEN GIRE

God knows the rhythm of my spirit and knows my heart thoughts.
He is as close as breathing.

The Rhythms of Life

How can we honor our God with our lives, the God who gives rain in both spring and autumn and maintains the rhythm of the seasons?

JEREMIAH 5:24 THE MESSAGE

At Home in His Love

Make your home in me just as I do in you. In the same way that a branch can't bear grapes by itself but only by being joined to the vine, you can't bear fruit unless you are joined with me.

I am the Vine, you are the branches. When you're joined with me and I with you, the relation intimate and organic, the harvest is sure to be abundant. Separated, you can't produce a thing....

But if you make yourselves at home with me and my words are at home in you, you can be sure that whatever you ask will be listened to and acted upon.... I've loved you the way my Father has loved me. Make yourselves at home in my love.

JOHN 15:4-9 THE MESSAGE

At Home in His Love

*This is and has been the Father's work from the beginning—
to bring us into the home of His heart.*

GEORGE MACDONALD

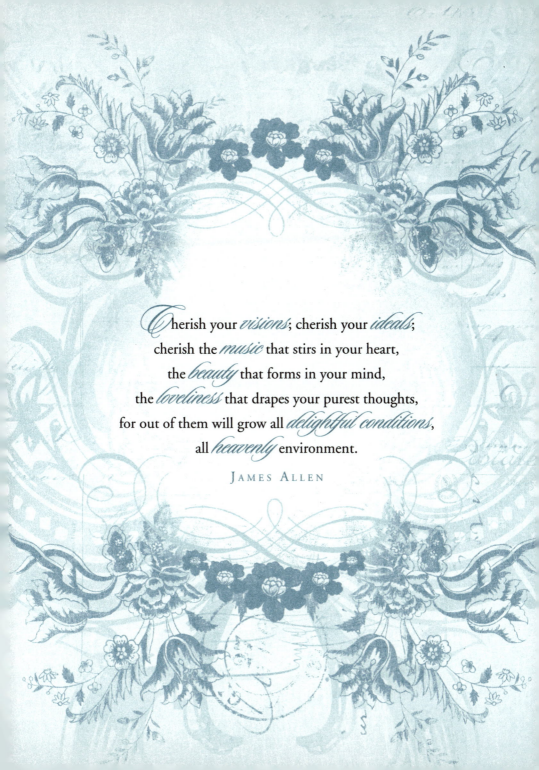

Cherish your *visions*; cherish your *ideals*;
cherish the *music* that stirs in your heart,
the *beauty* that forms in your mind,
the *loveliness* that drapes your purest thoughts,
for out of them will grow all *delightful conditions*,
all *heavenly* environment.

JAMES ALLEN

Countless Beauties

From the world we see, hear, and touch, we behold inspired visions that reveal God's glory. In the sun's light, we catch warm rays of grace and glimpse His eternal design. In the birds' song, we hear His voice and it reawakens our desire for Him. At the wind's touch, we feel His Spirit and sense our eternal existence.

May God give you eyes to see beauty only the heart can understand.

It is one of the beautiful compensations of this life that no person can sincerely try to help another without helping himself.

RALPH WALDO EMERSON

All the world is an utterance of the Almighty. Its countless beauties, its exquisite adaptations, all speak to you of Him.

PHILLIPS BROOKS

Countless Beauties

Worship the Lord in the beauty of holiness.

Psalm 96:9 nkjv

Glorious Riches

I pray that out of His glorious riches He may strengthen you with power through His Spirit in your inner being, so that Christ may dwell in your hearts through faith.

And I pray that you, being rooted and established in love, may have power, together with all the saints, to grasp how wide and long and high and deep is the love of Christ, and to know this love that surpasses knowledge—that you may be filled to the measure of all the fullness of God.

Now to Him who is able to do immeasurably more than all we ask or imagine, according to His power that is at work within us, to Him be glory in the church and in Christ Jesus throughout all generations, for ever and ever! Amen.

EPHESIANS 3:16-21 NIV

Glorious Riches

> *Lord...give me only Your love and Your grace. With this I am rich enough, and I have no more to ask.*
>
> IGNATIUS OF LOYOLA

Praise Overflows

All enjoyment spontaneously overflows into praise.... The world rings with praise.... I think we delight to praise what we enjoy because the praise not merely expresses but completes the enjoyment; it is the appointed consummation.

C. S. Lewis

Does not all nature around me praise God? If I were silent, I should be an exception to the universe. Does not the thunder praise Him as it rolls like drums in the march of the God of armies?... Does not the lightning write His name in letters of fire? Has not the whole earth a voice? And...can I silent be?

C. H. Spurgeon

God's pursuit of praise from us and our pursuit of pleasure in Him are one and the same pursuit. God's quest to be glorified and our quest to be satisfied reach their goal in this one experience: our delight in God which overflows in praise.

John Piper

Praise Overflows

O sing to the Lord a new song! Sing to the Lord, all the earth.

PSALM 96:1 NKJV

An Inner Place

Retire from the world each day to some private spot.... Stay in the secret place till the surrounding noises begin to fade out of your heart and a sense of God's presence envelops you.... Listen for the inward Voice till you learn to recognize it.... Give yourself to God and then be what and who you are without regard to what others think.... Learn to pray inwardly every moment.

A. W. TOZER

The impetus of God's love comes from within Himself, to share with us His life and love. It is a beautiful, eternal gift, held out to us in the hands of love. All we have to do is say "Yes!"

JOHN POWELL

I will remember that when I give Him my heart, God chooses to live within me—body and soul. He fills all of the empty places, His very Spirit inside of me.

An Inner Place

Be beautiful inside, in your hearts, with the lasting charm of a gentle and quiet spirit which is so precious to God.

1 Peter 3:4 TLB

Life Itself

God, your God, will cut away the thick calluses on your heart and your children's hearts, freeing you to love God, your God, with your whole heart and soul and live, really live....

And you will make a new start, listening obediently to God, keeping all His commandments that I'm commanding you today. God, your God, will outdo Himself in making things go well for you....

Love God, your God. Walk in His ways. Keep His commandments, regulations, and rules so that you will live, really live, live exuberantly, blessed by God.... Love God, your God, listening obediently to Him, firmly embracing Him. Oh yes, He is life itself.

DEUTERONOMY 30:6, 8-9, 16, 20 THE MESSAGE

Life Itself

*I asked God for all things that I might enjoy life.
He gave me life that I might enjoy all things.*

There are two kinds of people in the world:
those who come into a room and say,
"Here I am!" and those who come in and say,

"Ah, there you are!"